CPSIA information can be obtained
at www.ICGtesting.com
Printed in the USA
LVHW052326081019
633649LV00009B/327/P

9 780368 973444